Do you have ideas for subjects which could be included in this exciting and innovative series? Could your company benefit from close involvement with a forthcoming title?

Please contact David Grant Publishing Limited
80 Ridgeway, Pembury, Tunbridge Wells, Kent TN2 4EZ
Tel/Fax +44 (0)1892 822886
Email GRANTPUB@aol.com
with your ideas or suggestions.

HOW TO PUBLICISE YOUR BUSINESS (AND YOURSELF!)

Forthcoming titles in this series will include

- *Win–Win Negotiation*
- *Coping Under Pressure*
- *How to Wow an Audience*
- *Coping With Office Politics*
- *How to Pay Less Tax*
- *Building Your Self-image*
- *Making the Most of Meetings*
- *Key Account Management*

HOW TO PUBLICISE YOUR BUSINESS (AND YOURSELF!)

Mike Park

60 Minutes Success Skills Series

Copyright © David Grant Publishing Limited 2000

First published 2000 by
David Grant Publishing Limited
80 Ridgeway
Pembury
Kent TN2 4EZ
United Kingdom

03 02 01   10 9 8 7 6 5 4 3 2 1

60 Minutes Success Skills Series is an imprint of
David Grant Publishing Limited

All rights reserved. Except for the quotation of short passages for the purposes of criticism and review, no part of this publication may be reproduced, stored in a retrieval system, or transmitted, in any form or by any means, electronic, mechanical, photocopying, recording or otherwise, without the prior permission of the publisher.

British Library Cataloguing in Publication Data
A CIP catalogue record for this book is available from the British Library

ISBN 1-901306-21-6
Cover design: Liz Rowe

Text design: Graham Rich
Editor: Kim Latham
Production coordinator: Paul Stringer
Edited and Typeset in Futura by Kate Williams
Printed and bound in Great Britain by
T.J. International Ltd, Padstow, Cornwall

This book is printed on acid-free paper

The publishers accept no responsibility for any investment or financial decisions made on the basis of the information in this book. Readers are advised always to consult a qualified financial adviser.

All names mentioned in the text have been changed to protect the identity of the business people involved. Any resemblance to existing companies or people is entirely coincidental.

Contents

Welcome: About *How to Publicise Your Business*   7

Chapter 1: You, Your Market, Your Image   9
    Define your unique qualities
    Know your market and customers
    Avoid wastage in marketing
    A little research goes a long way
    Understand the visual image
    Get the most from a graphic designer
    Develop the right visual style

Chapter 2: Grab the Media's Attention   15
    Why you should bother with media relations
    Select the right types of media for your business
    Prepare news stories about your organisation
    Treat journalists as customers
    Good photographs make all the difference
    Get the most from broadcasting media

Chapter 3: Improving Promotional Punch   27
    Customers are your best sales weapon
    Mobilise customers to support your marketing
    Discover ready-made press publicity opportunities
    Convey your message in editorial format
    Get someone else to help pay for your advertorials
    Sponsorship can be part of your marketing mix
    Exploit your investment
    The Internet is a valuable marketing tool
    Create a web site

Chapter 4: Tricks of the Trade 37
Get the best value from advertising
Making the exhibition decision
Get the most from show participation
Exploit face-to-face communications
Make a success of speaker opportunities
Use your products as prizes
Get the most from media competitions
An open day can be a public relations coup
Decide if an open day is right for you

Chapter 5: See the Results 47
Simple and effective ways to measure publicity success
Lessons from case histories

WELCOME

ABOUT *HOW TO PUBLICISE YOUR BUSINESS*

Can you really learn enough in just one hour to help you effectively publicise your business and yourself? The answer is a resounding "Yes". This book provides you with a blueprint which will point you in all the right directions, and gives you lots of tips and advice that will help you get the maximum exposure and thereby improve your business performance.

The 60 Minutes Success Skills Series is written for people with neither the time nor the patience to trawl through acres of jargon and management-speak. Like all the books in the series, *How to Publicise Your Business* has been written in the belief that you can learn all you really need to know quickly and without hassle. The aim is to distil the essential, practical advice you can use straight away.

How to use this book

The message here is "It's OK to skim". Feel free to flick through to find the help you need most. This book is a collection of hands-on tips which will help you to spot any shortcomings you might have and show you how to turn them into strengths.

Divided into five chapters, *How to Publicise Your Business* deals with all the key issues that face every company looking to make a name for themselves and reach all the potential customers in their market. Take 60 minutes to find out how to get your products and services noticed by a wider audience. And it needn't be expensive.

As you read through the book, you will come across lots of tips and practical advice on how to make a big impact when promoting your image. If you're really pushed for time, you could start by just going straight to any of the boxed features, which will ask you either to think about a problem or to do something about it and then give you some ideas.

GOOD LUCK!

YOU, YOUR MARKET, YOUR IMAGE — Chapter 1

Coming up in this chapter

Define your unique qualities
Know your market and customers
Avoid wastage in marketing
A little research goes a long way
Understand the visual image
Get the most from a graphic designer
Develop the right visual style

DECIDE WHAT'S SPECIAL ABOUT YOU

> Are you ever at your wits' end in trying to attract customers who you're sure should be doing business with you, rather than your rivals?

You can be absolutely certain of one thing: you are *different*. Even if you make the same product or offer the same service as your competitors, there will be something unique to you that will appeal to your customers. This is what you must define at the outset and then concentrate on that difference in your publicity.

Avis, the vehicle hire firm, made a virtue of being second to its biggest competitor by trumpeting "We try harder". British Airways decided from its research that it was "The world's favourite airline". These strong and memorable messages differentiated the two firms from all their competitors and got customers to listen — and buy. Virgin has decided that what sets its diverse range of companies apart, wherever they compete, is the personality of its founder, Richard Branson.

> Be prepared to think laterally about your own special image.

HOW TO PUBLICISE YOUR BUSINESS (AND YOURSELF!)

TRUST
CONFIDENCE
INNOVATIVE

> *" My problem was getting anybody to be interested in what I was offering. All my rivals seemed to be competing on price alone. I thought it was a commodity market until I got talking to people and realised that it was trust that made me different from the rest. "*
> – **Floyd Hamilton, network cabling installer**

A baker thought it would be a hilarious idea to exploit the pun "Knead the Dough", without realising the joke was on him. It appeared to be a begging message and certainly said nothing about the product to encourage customers.

ACT!

Get together with your colleagues, family, friends or some customers, and "brainstorm" unique features about your company that set you apart from the rest.

Here are some examples to which you should add the results of your brainstorm and then rate each factor on a scale of 1 (poor) to 5 (excellent). Be realistic and honest, and don't list too many — that will only complicate your sales message.

- ❏ Price
- ☑ Reliability
- ☑ Results
- ❏ Understanding
- ☑ Flexibility
- ❏ Fun
- ❏ No frills
- ❏ All-rounder
- ☑ Value
- ❏ Durability
- ☑ Location
- ❏ Stability
- ❏ Tradition
- ❏ Seriousness
- ❏ High-tech
- ☑ Specialist
- ❏ Quality
- ❏ Delivery
- ❏ Trust
- ❏ Helpfulness
- ❏ Modernity
- ❏ Prestige
- ❏ Simplicity

Any others?

S
CLOSE THE LOOP
RE-USE

A publicity message encapsulates what it is about a company that makes it special.

ACT!

Summarise in a statement of no more than five or six words (fewer if your difference is simple) what you think is unique about your company. *Remember, this is actually a sales message that must mean something to your customers, not just to you. Use it at every opportunity in all your publicity material.*

YOU, YOUR MARKET, YOUR IMAGE

> *" Commercial art is part of the communications business, so in devising my unique proposition, I found out that what people wanted from me was straight talk, not the kind of arty jargon that deters customers from using designers. "*
> — **Sunil Gupta, graphic designer**
> (Sunil's message is "Eyes that speak your language.")

Don't rush into print with your sales message until you have generated some feedback from the people to whom it is intended to appeal: your existing and potential customers. Then fine-tune the words if necessary. That way you will avoid making the expensive mistake of being too subjective.

DEFINE YOUR MARKET

Assuming that your product would appeal to the people you visualised as customers, have you ever got around to forming a precise picture of who they are, where they live or operate and whether you can reach them?

What you must try to achieve is an exact fix on the one or more groups of people who are going to be your customers: their age bands, sex, where they live, social status or, if selling to businesses, what and who influences the decision to buy.

> *" What a difference a little analysis has made to my marketing! Instead of generating enquiries from people I couldn't deliver to, I'm now more realistic. Using databases and distributors covering rural areas in one region at a time has meant big savings and raised the sales hit rate. "*
> — **Darren Richardson, wood-burning stoves supplier**

Research is everything in marketing — but market research can be prohibitively expensive. So, if you are at all unsure of which audiences to concentrate on in your publicity, test your product or service with focus groups of the people you originally had in mind. These small meetings are inexpensive and can be

HOW TO PUBLICISE YOUR BUSINESS (AND YOURSELF!)

organised locally for up to six or seven people. Structure the meeting to examine the benefits of what you are offering. The results will give you a reliable guide to future promotion.

> **Don't waste time trying to reach people who will never or rarely buy your product.**

Examine the examples of customer definitions listed, then rate them as high, medium, low or zero priority.

Where are they?
- ○ International
- ○ National
- ○ Local
- ○ Regional or state-wide
- ○ Urban
- ○ Suburban
- ○ Rural

Who are they?
- ○ Age
  - Over 60
  - 35–59
  - 20–34
  - Teenage
  - Children
- ○ Gender
- ○ Social status/class
  - Upper middle/professional
  - Lower middle/white collar
  - Lower middle/skilled
  - Working/unskilled

  - Mothers
  - Fathers
  - Married/no children
  - Single

  - Housewives
  - Home owners

  - Ethnic group relevance

Businesses
- ○ Size
  - Large (500+ staff)
  - Medium (over 50)
  - Small (up to 50)
- ○ Buyers: professional/part-time
- ○ Trade/distributors
- ○ Consultants
- ○ Financial executives
- ○ Directors/VPs
- ○ Secretaries/PAs
- ○ Technicians
- ○ Administrators

YOU, YOUR MARKET, YOUR IMAGE

CREATE YOUR VISUAL IMAGE

> Do you ever think that your business stationery, brochures, leaflets etc. look very ordinary? Are you really satisfied that they reflect what you think about your business?

Whatever you produce will say something about your company to your customers. Just as talking to someone in a particular tone of voice will generate a specific response, so the visual tone of printed materials and signs will also evoke an impression about your organisation.

Consult an expert — a graphic designer — before you start spending money on an image that may not work for you. Ask colleagues, friends or local business groups for recommendations.

The most important element in company print is your *logo*, which is the style of typeface in which your firm's name always appears. You may also wish to commission a *symbol* or *trade mark*. But make sure you convey the right image to your customers. A sports shop should not give the impression of a funeral director — and vice versa!

> *Your logo is your advertisement*. Always use it and never change the design on different elements of print. Your "look", or corporate identity, must be consistent.

Go back to the list of your unique qualities that you created at the start of this chapter, and make sure your designer understands the meaning. Then ask for two or three alternatives to choose from, along with the most economical print option. If you think you can buy print cheaper yourself, fine — you don't then pay the designer's mark-up.

> Decide which of the following printed matter you will need:
> - ❏ Letterheads   ❏ Invoices   ❏ Compliments slips
> - ❏ Business cards   ❏ Envelopes   ❏ Parcel stickers

thirteen

HOW TO PUBLICISE YOUR BUSINESS (AND YOURSELF!)

- ☐ Order forms
- ☐ Leaflets
- ☐ Catalogues
- ☐ Packaging
- ☐ Displays
- ☐ Estimate forms
- ☐ Brochures
- ☐ Posters
- ☐ Point-of-sale
- ☐ Spec sheets
- ☐ Folders
- ☐ Newsletters
- ☐ Signs

> ❝ I have to admit that I was fairly cynical about corporate identity. I regarded it as just another example of management jargon. Then a business adviser asked me to focus my mind seriously on what impression we were communicating to the market with our thoughtlessly produced print and livery. It didn't take long before I was on the phone to a couple of design firms! ❞
> — **Peter Couldwell, haulage contractor**

A recruitment agency decided that the best way to symbolise the business of putting people in touch with each other was a handshake emblem. Having spent a great deal of money on the idea, the agency gradually realised that the concept applied to many other service or people businesses, too. Everyone, it seemed, had used the first idea that came into their heads.

Two of the most readily recognised trade marks in the world were produced by two very different firms with quite different images to convey: Ford and Apple Computer. The Ford logo is based on Henry Ford's signature and was intended to symbolise to the world the company founder's personal vision. The Apple trade mark – a multicoloured striped apple with a bite in the side – conveys the freshness and freedom of thinking always associated with the firm, serving it well throughout the ups and downs of business fortune.

Think about how you respond to the world-beating logos of Coca-Cola or McDonald's. Imagine how familiarity with yours could help your business succeed.

GRAB THE MEDIA'S ATTENTION — Chapter 2

Coming up in this chapter

Why you should bother with media relations
Select the right types of media for your business
Prepare news stories about your organisation
Treat journalists as customers
Good photographs make all the difference
Get the most from broadcasting media

THE FIRST STEPS IN MEDIA PUBLICITY

Does it annoy you when you see your competitors written about in the press, especially when your organisation makes a better product and you have more sensible things to say?

The previous chapter dealt with defining what you want to say, who you are going to say it to, and how you are going to look. Now it is time to examine the media (newspapers, magazines, radio, TV and their "on-line" Internet versions) that you want to carry your "story".

Remember, we are not yet talking about advertising. We are focusing on getting the media interested in writing about your organisation editorially: in articles and features. This involves understanding the way journalists work and, in effect, treating them as if they were customers.

Any salesperson will tell you that word-of-mouth recommendation is the best sales tool. And media coverage is like word-of-mouth amplified. It is seen as an independent assessment (unlike advertising or direct mail, which the audience recognises as a company talking about itself).

HOW TO PUBLICISE YOUR BUSINESS (AND YOURSELF!)

" My cable firm had a great but simple idea for storing and displaying cables – a specially designed bracket. We decided to promote this new product editorially in our customers' trade press and we got some great coverage. Then we mailed copies of the best articles to potential new customers, with a covering letter, and exploited the apparent independence of media stories to improve the credibility of this direct mail shot. Result?
The best response in our history. "
– Gerrard Hovell, POS Perfect

HOW TO RESEARCH THE MEDIA

Your local library will have directories from which you can extract useful information about particular publications. Or ask the advertising departments of the media you are interested in for a media pack, which will contain independently audited figures on the people who read them and a list of subjects to be covered in future issues. The pack will also contain a copy of the publication, so you can judge for yourself the type of story and picture you need to prepare to get into print.

The result of this minimal research will be your *media directory* – your "bible" containing the basic information you will need to work with the media who will help you reach your customers.

" It's the new age of marketing for professional services. So when I sat down and studied the range of magazines and newspaper sections covering my field, I was amazed at the opportunities they represented to reach the market. I simply hadn't appreciated the diversity of media that our customers read. "
– Natasha Semple, lawyer

Bearing in mind the list of areas and customer types you identified earlier, choose the media types applicable to your market and write down the name, editor (or specialist writer), contact details (phone and fax numbers, email address) and the submission deadlines of the actual media you will be dealing with in your publicity programme.
If you need wide coverage, consider the news agencies who distribute good news stories they receive to all media.

GRAB THE MEDIA'S ATTENTION

- ❏ National daily or Sunday newspapers
- ❏ National television
- ❏ National radio
- ❏ National consumer magazines
- ❏ Regional daily or Sunday newspapers
- ❏ Regional television
- ❏ Local weekly newspapers
- ❏ Local radio
- ❏ County magazines
- ❏ National business journals
- ❏ Your trade press
- ❏ Technical press
- ❏ Customer trade press
- ❏ Local business journals
- ❏ Customer house journals
- ❏ Freelance writers
- ❏ Internet, or online, journals
- ❏ News agencies

Press releases

A news story that you write about your own organisation is called a press release.

> Have you sent material to the press that has never been used, despite the fact that you spent time carefully and painstakingly putting the facts together?

If the average news editor had five pounds for every unusable press release they received, they would never need to work again.

Many releases open with "XYZ Ltd are pleased to announce..." and then ramble to no particular conclusion. Others start with a ridiculously overstated (and unsubstantiated) claim like "XYZ Ltd have annihilated the competition with a quantum leap in DIY technology...", followed by unintelligible jargon punctuated with too many exclamation marks.

So let's look at how you go about preparing a press release that will attract the attention of a news editor.

You have already decided in the first chapter what sets your company and your offering apart from the competition. When you launch a new product or service, for example, that in itself is a news story because your target media should be interested in what constitutes a "first". Anything that you or your product alone possess, the unique characteristics which appeal to your customers, will be of interest.

> **Look at the list of your product/service's unique features, and fill in the gaps in the opening sentence of your own press release:**
>
> "A new product/service was launched today by [your company] that for the first time enables [describe your customers] to [summarise the benefit]."
>
> **You may also have done some market research that establishes the need for your product. Facts are what the press thrive on. If you have them available, fill in the gaps of the second part of your launch story:**
>
> "Research conducted by [your company] showed that [the need for your product/service]. This need has now been met by [your company], whose customers will benefit from [expand on benefit of your product]."
>
> **Now all that is needed is a quote from a trial or prospective customer, an objective comment of your own and details of price and availability. Add the date and particulars for further information and you have just written the press release that will launch your new product to your media directory.**

Post, fax or email the press release to the contacts in your media directory. If it is important that your story is not published before a certain date or time, type the word "Embargoed" at the top with that date or time. Or wait until you have organised a press meeting. This process is explained below.

Find time to follow up the most important journalists. But never call to say "Did you get my press release?" The press absolutely hate this approach. The only reason to call them is to offer an interview, a photograph, or some special angle of particular interest to their readers. And have the courtesy to ask at the outset if this is a good time to call – imagine how you react when pestered while trying to meet a deadline.

GRAB THE MEDIA'S ATTENTION

> *" I found the idea of preparing a press release a bit daunting at first. It seemed like a lot of work – but it made me think objectively about why anybody should want to come to my garden centre. I thought back to the time when I originally started this business and how I knew I could provide better products and better value than my former employers. And I really had first-hand knowledge of what gardeners were looking for. So I decided that I had a good story to tell after all. "*
> – **Nicholas Prendergast, garden centre owner**

Do you fail to see the point of sending a specially written piece of information to a journalist? Having gone to the trouble and expense of writing and printing a brochure, do you think they should do a story based on that?

The whole point of working with journalists is to give them a credible and factual story which they are most likely to run with. There is no chance that they will try to rework the sales pitch of a brochure text into something suitable for their readers. If they can't get a story pre-digested from you, they certainly will from the competition!

How to write a press release

1. *The subject:* State your business in the first sentence. Anyone reading your release must immediately be made aware of the hard news fact you are communicating.
2. *Your business:* Don't overestimate public interest in your company. You have to persuade them why you are special by stating the benefits of dealing with you.
3. *Location:* The media need contact phone numbers, so always include them at the top of the release, especially if they are different from your standard business particulars.
4. *What's special?:* A "first", unique product advantages, a service never offered before, or unusual cicumstances: all of these attract press attention. Think – would an outsider really find this interesting?

HOW TO PUBLICISE YOUR BUSINESS (AND YOURSELF!)

5. *Sales talk:* Don't oversell in the text of the release. Remember, you are not writing an advert. If your release smacks of sales patter it will end up in the editor's bin to join the hundreds of handouts they get every week.
6. *Detail:* Don't worry if you can't include product or company details without breaking up the flow of the story. Don't make it complicated. Put details in "bullet-point" form on a separate sheet headed "Notes to Editors".
7. *Quotes:* A customer or influential third party endorsing your product or service is much more credible than you saying it yourself.
8. *Layout:* Remember to leave wide margins and type the release in double spacing to enable easy "subbing" by the news editor. Put the date of release at the top along with a contact name for further information. A home telephone number may also be appreciated by the press.

Meeting the press

Press meetings are called to give the publicist (you) a chance to sell their story face-to-face through a dialogue that enables the subject to be treated in depth. After you have expressed your story in your own words in your press release, you can introduce yourself in person to the journalists who are most important to you. This will also give them the chance to get their own angles on your news, but still based on your press release.

Unless you have a blockbuster wonder-product of national interest, don't invite all your media together. The smaller the group the bigger the result. Also, consider meeting the most important journalists one at a time.

Select the journalists you will invite, and the media they work for – and split them into groups of up to four at different times of the day according to their deadlines and competing interests.

GRAB THE MEDIA'S ATTENTION

Here are two typical examples of groups of non-competing media:

Example 1:
National newspaper
Local weekly newspaper
Customer trade journal
National business journal

Example 2:
National radio
Regional daily newspaper
Women's magazine
Your trade journal

[handwritten: Contact Eve News]

- ❏ Make sure your occasion doesn't clash with another media event on the same day – check with an editor first.
- ❏ Write an invitation letter, follow up on the phone and confirm the time and place in writing.
- ❏ Use your own premises for the meetings, unless they are really unsuitable or a long way from a major city.
- ❏ Rehearse in front of colleagues or friends – and get them to dream up some awkward questions.
- ❏ Keep apart competing journalists from the same media category.
- ❏ Don't bore them with a long presentation. Fifteen minutes is plenty, with 30 to 45 minutes for discussion.
- ❏ Make sure you avoid meeting on the day they go to press.
- ❏ Be hospitable but limit the alcohol. Don't pretend to be The Ritz.
- ❏ Always make sure you stick to the simple plus-points about your enterprise and your product.
- ❏ Don't mention your competitors voluntarily.
- ❏ Give journalists access to the product and – even better – a customer.
- ❏ Make a note of any further information or action they require and be sure to follow up.

Don't feel you need to fill the whole day. Be satisfied if you get most of your important media to attend. Others can be contacted by phone.

Is taking all this trouble worth it, especially considering how unreliable the press can be? Does pandering to a load of hacks who want the story on a plate seem a waste of time when you have a business to run?

twenty-one

HOW TO PUBLICISE YOUR BUSINESS (AND YOURSELF!)

Meeting the press does take effort. Revise your press lists constantly, according to the acceptances you get. There will inevitably be some "no-shows" and last-minute cancellations. But be flexible and patient – remember the priceless nature of media coverage of your business mission!

> *Meeting journalists for the first time was an invigorating experience once I'd got past the suspicious stage. The knowledgeable questions some of them asked made me feel they were part of my industry – and on my side. Even the natural cynics among them sharpened my wits. The dialogue helped me think laterally about my business strategy and ways of selling product benefits. The investment of my time was justified by the long-term press relationships developed as well as the short-term publicity.*
> – **David Reshevsky, Internet service provider**

ACT!

Prepare a press kit to give to journalists. It should contain:
- ❑ Your press release.
- ❑ A single typed sheet giving the background on your company, and who runs it.
- ❑ One or more photographs (see next section): of you, your premises (only if interesting) or the product (preferably in the hands of a customer).
- ❑ A leaflet or brochure containing product/service details and specification.

Don't spend money printing special folders (unless you already have something suitable). A clear plastic folder is perfectly OK.

Photo files

A good picture not only increases the chances of your story getting into the press, it also makes your message leap off the page to sell your company. But do bear in mind that sometimes the media prefer to use their own photographer.

GRAB THE MEDIA'S ATTENTION

Have you spent money on photographs for a brochure and sent these to the press to illustrate a story, only to find they were hardly used, or totally ignored, possibly along with the text?

The trouble with brochure pictures is that they tend to have insufficient "life" for press use, especially if they are amateur shots. You will need to use a professional photographer to get the quality needed for good press reproduction – particularly for technical work. Ask the picture editor of your local newspaper for a recommendation.

Get quotes and ask to see the work of a selection of photographers. Then write down the details of the best two candidates, along with their charges for a photo session and costs of prints and colour transparencies.

Getting the most from press photographs

- ❏ Write a short caption that summarises the story. Add a contact name and phone number.
- ❏ Check the types of picture that get printed in your target media and whether they use colour.
- ❏ If possible, try to get a person in the shot.
- ❏ Send 6" × 4" or 8" × 6" prints; colour transparencies should not be smaller than 2.25" square.
- ❏ Passport photos make people look like morons.
- ❏ Mail photos in hard-backed envelopes.
- ❏ Pictures should have plenty of contrast to give depth when printed.
- ❏ Don't forget, to be a winner, the picture must tell the story creatively, so think about the possibilities of computerised compilation techniques.

❝ *The creativity and attention to detail shown by the photographer recommended by my main trade magazine were very impressive. He had ideas I would never have thought of in a professional lifetime – even though the machines we made were my own brainchild!*

HOW TO PUBLICISE YOUR BUSINESS (AND YOURSELF!)

Not only did the pictures get published, but I decided to scrap the old shots used in my literature and substituted these much more lively ones in the next reprint. "
– **Christophe LaGrande, packaging machinery manufacturer**

The publicity people for PC direct sales firm Gateway 2000 hit upon a radically new idea to brighten up dull computer photography. They exploited the company's black and white packaging by placing the boxes in a field, and modified some boxes to look like Friesian cows. Company boss Ted Waitt posed among them, dressed casually in keeping with the made-up rural setting. The result was one of the most frequently published and remembered shots in the world's most competitive and over-hyped industry.

Photo call notification

Here is an example of how to summon photographers (and, if the story is strong enough, camera crews) from the media. Treat it as a template to create your own photo call notification, using your company stationery.

PHOTO CALL

Date: Tuesday, XX November, 20XX

Time: 10.30 a.m.

Place: BRIAN'S BICYCLE SHOP, 22 The Pavement, Yourtown

Background:
   60 year-old Brian Benzie, owner of Brian's Bicycle Shop, is setting out to be the oldest man to reach the top of Ben Nevis on a bicycle – but not just any bicycle.
   Brian's mount is a 100-year-old penny farthing model which has been used as the shop's sign, and which Brian has painstakingly restored.
   A Scotsman through-and-through, Brian will make the attempt attired in a kilt and highland jacket.

ENDS

For further information, phone Brian Benzie on XXX XXXX

GRAB THE MEDIA'S ATTENTION

GETTING YOUR MESSAGE ON THE AIR

Do you often feel that the stories broadcast on local radio are pathetic? Would you like to give them something more interesting about your own company activities – like charity sponsorship – but you're worried about being interviewed and what it entails?

Whatever sphere of radio or TV you might participate in, you are extremely unlikely to bump into a hostile interviewer – unless you blatantly try to exploit the medium as a sales tool. Grillings are reserved generally for politicians or fat-cat business people.

Your first thought must be whether the press release you sent your local TV or radio station is interesting enough for them to consider broadcasting. In the case of radio, they will either send someone to interview you or ask you to come to the studio. TV is much harder to attract because they have less time to fill and need something highly visual if they are going to the expense of sending a camera team (a relatively rare occurrence).

Attracting broadcast media is made easier if you match the type of programme to your story: e.g. new product and branch launches or employment stories for news bulletins; fun, general or human interest stories for breakfast or magazine shows.

> **"** Television and radio are highly seductive media for the aspiring publicist, but they can be either a triumph or a disaster, depending on whether you know how to work with broadcasters. Television and radio interviewers are not necessarily there to do you any favours. Why should they? Their prime concern – they will like to point out – is to protect the interests of the public, so trying to exploit an interview as a sales opportunity will soon be exposed by a journalist so inclined. **"**
> – **Jim Henderson, regional TV news editor**

twenty-five

HOW TO PUBLICISE YOUR BUSINESS (AND YOURSELF!)

When MGM, whose roaring lion is arguably the best recognised image in the film industry, decided to launch a new venture, their PR firm sensibly wanted to exploit the big-cat branding. The idea of using a lion cub to symbolise MGM's new venture was irresistible. It went wrong when, after the media, including TV crews, had been summoned to a photo call, the animal agency turned up – with a *tiger* cub! If you want to work with animals (or children) choose your supplier very carefully.

Ask yourself these questions to decide whether radio and/or TV are right for your organisation:

- Are these media in your media directory?
- Did you get a media pack from them (so you know their audience)?
- Would you be happy to be interviewed live in a studio or on the phone?
- Would you be happy to take part in a recorded interview at your own premises?
- If not, would you be prepared to pay for media training? (A half-day session should be sufficient. Check rates from lists printed in PR journals.)

Alternatively, you can create your own TV or radio tape which is made and distributed by a professional studio whom you can consult. But the costs can be high: big bucks for radio and mega bucks for TV. If you think your story can justify this sort of treatment, get a recommendation from your local radio or TV station and ask for quotes and evaluated examples of their work.

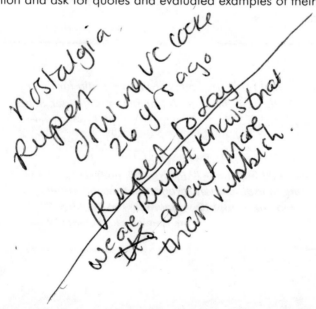

IMPROVING PROMOTIONAL PUNCH — Chapter 3

Coming up in this chapter

Customers are your best sales weapon
Mobilise customers to support your marketing
Discover ready-made press publicity opportunities
Convey your message in editorial format
Get someone else to help pay for your advertorials
Sponsorship can be part of your marketing mix
Exploit your investment
The Internet is a valuable marketing tool
Create a web site

HOW CUSTOMERS CAN GET YOU NOTICED

Are you too busy taking orders and getting the product delivered to find out what benefit the customer actually derives from your efforts?

In Chapter 2 we said that media relations is word-of-mouth recommendation amplified. Word-of-mouth is the salesperson's best weapon – and case histories are the best ammunition: the most credible form of publicity, not just for sales literature but also for press coverage.

To decide on the right approach, look at the criteria listed here. See which ones apply to you and then call your first friendly customer.

○ You are happy to spend time on this activity which may involve you interviewing customers yourself (although this can be done in a 15-minute phone call).
○ The customer is willing to take part in publicity (tell them it makes them look efficient/progressive/clever).
○ Their use of your product is typical of the benefits you want to sell to others.

HOW TO PUBLICISE YOUR BUSINESS (AND YOURSELF!)

- ○ You know one or more journals who will publish this sort of material.
- ○ The journal is happy for you to supply an article with photographs (ask the features editor about content and style), or...
- ○ ...the journal would rather cover the case history themselves after you have sent them a brief outline.
- ○ You are willing to make sure the customer sees the text before publication.

Including customer case histories in your publicity programme can also promote the benefits of your product or service to an entire market – possibly in a single press article! You may never be able to get coverage in certain types of magazine you want to get into, since they only write about users, not suppliers or vendors. But frequently, they publish feature articles that are liberally illustrated by case histories. This is your chance to strike.

In preparing a case history, it pays to be objective, so get an intelligent outsider to actually interview your customer (on the phone will be fine). It relieves you of this task and will enable a fresh mind to be applied to the relationship you have with the customer and the benefits they get from dealing with you. Moreover, it is easier for a third party to ask a customer the questions listed below – and the customer is more likely to be forthcoming.

> *" Developing case histories with customers not only strengthened my long-term relationships with them, I also discovered in far greater depth what my lubricants were used for and why we were better than our competitors. In one instance, I actually found out for the first time that my organisation had been promoted to preferred supplier status! "*
> **– Gerry Reuben, sales director, industrial oil products**

First write to your customer asking for permission to write a case study. Don't talk about press publicity at this stage. When the story is finished, and they can see how good it is, discuss the benefits to both of you of media coverage.

IMPROVING PROMOTIONAL PUNCH

Here is a typical list of questions to be answered:

- How long have they been dealing with your company?
- How did they come to appoint you? For example: new project, previous supplier performance, recommendation, new technology, etc.
- What products/services do they receive from your company, and what applications do they use them for?
- What do they regard as different or special about your company's approach?
- What do they perceive as the benefits/results of using your products/services?

Once you have absorbed Chapters 1 and 2, which establish the credentials of your enterprise, build up a steady stream of continuing publicity based on your customers.

> Keep the contents of each case history simple, contained on a single sheet of A4 paper, along these lines:
> - **The situation:** customer's type of business, markets, speciality, their need for your product or service.
> - **The solution:** how you work with the customer to solve their problem or improve their business.
> - **The result:** the quantified benefits to the customer, including enhancing your customer contact's own professional life. Finish with a customer quote.

Remember to make sure each time that you obtain your customer's agreement to the final text *in writing*. This is essential for text that is going to be published.

❝ *Several case study customers were quick to see the publicity potential for their own businesses and readily agreed to my sending press releases about the story of our solution applied to their technology. The view of one particular client was typical: hiring our company to support their research and development showed how they were leaders in innovation in their own industry. They actually thanked us for helping them get recognition.* ❞
   – **Martin Huckerby, supplier to the construction industry**

HOW TO PUBLICISE YOUR BUSINESS (AND YOURSELF!)

Build up enough opportunities to develop case histories to enable you to concentrate only on those that exemplify the contribution you make to the sectors, or size of customer, that you most want to target in your marketing.

EXPLOITING SPECIAL FEATURES AND SURVEYS

> Do you ever find yourself reading major feature articles, in the trade press or even national newspapers, that cover your sphere of business but that you didn't know were going to appear? Instead of your competitors supplying information to journalists, should it have been you?

Sometimes, the media in your media directory will publish a special feature (or they may describe it as a report or survey) on the business field that you operate in. The media packs discussed in Chapter 2 should contain the list for the current year.

Inevitably, though, these features are written by freelance writers hired by the journal. This is because full-time staff writers can rarely cope with the extra work. If you see a relevant advance feature flagged in your media pack, make sure you get the name of the freelance writer and present your case to him or her direct.

The normal essentials of good, hard information supplied on time apply equally here.

> Use the points below to ensure you are ready to take full advantage of the ready-made opportunities offered by special features:
> ❑ You have the latest feature lists for all your key media.
> ❑ You have the name of the features editor (or special reports editor) who will tell you who is writing the feature.
> ❑ You know the editorial deadlines.
> ❑ You have a case history or product story that will be of particular interest to the journal's readers.
> ❑ You have photographs to enhance your coverage – or you are willing to allow the journal's own photographer to visit you or a customer.

IMPROVING PROMOTIONAL PUNCH

> *Working with the freelancers who wrote these special features enabled me to uncover opportunities from all the other magazines they wrote for. The fact that I gave them the information they wanted first time round meant they came back to me when developing new features – without my having to call any features editors!*
> **– Yvonne Bradbury, recruitment consultant**

To exploit each opportunity, create a master list from your media pack advance features lists. Mark in your diary the date to approach the writer, ensuring it is well in advance of their copy deadline.

ADVERTORIALS GUARANTEE PUBLICITY

Have you seen those funny hybrid full-page features that contain an article supposedly written by the boss of a company, along with an advert for the same firm, and wondered how they managed that?

Advertorials, sometimes called advertising features, are a mixture of editorial matter and advertising space – and it's all paid for. Most magazines or newspapers in these revenue-conscious times will publish a special feature about your organisation, provided you place a minimum amount of advertising.

Although they don't have the full credibility of pure editorials written by reporters, advertorials are nevertheless an excellent way of guaranteeing the size of editorial you get – and the accuracy of the message you are communicating.

Check this list to see if advertorials can help your promotional cause:
- ❑ The journals in your media directory will publish advertorials (if you're not sure, call your contact).
- ❑ This is a way you can ensure publicity at a critical time, like an exhibition or product launch.

- ❏ You haven't got a fresh news story since the journal last covered your firm – and you need a publicity boost.
- ❏ You can support the feature with an advert you are happy with.
- ❏ You could reprint the feature for mail shots.

❝ The idea of buying space to write what I liked was pretty novel. I set about penning the article of my dreams, but had a colleague check it to prevent me going over the top! The experience of dealing in the verbal currency of a journalist opened my eyes to the type of job they do every day. As a result, I have been able to relate to them much better. Oh, and the phone hardly stopped for days after the advertorial was published. ❞
– Alan Boobyer, retail store manager

You don't always have to pay through the nose for advertorial coverage. A good trick is to get your suppliers to place adverts. You can lure them with a promise of a mention in the editorial part of the feature – which is written either by you or a freelance writer.

THE PROS AND CONS OF SPONSORSHIP

Do you like to know exactly what return you are getting for any investment? Does a lot of sponsorship seem to you to be an ego trip for the directors? Is it hard for you to see what else firms get out of this type of activity?

Companies sponsor sports, education, the arts or charities because of the goodwill and publicity this can generate. Also, an important element of sponsorship is the events they surround, which give the opportunity to entertain customers.

IMPROVING PROMOTIONAL PUNCH

Yes, sponsorship can be expensive, so small businesses, for example, should stick to opportunities like local soccer or basketball leagues, hospitals, schools or theatres. And you must be sure of value for money.

> Answer these questions to decide whether sponsorship is right for your company:
>
> ❏ Will significant numbers of your current or potential customers be either spectators or participants?
> ❏ Are any of your competitors successfully involved in sponsorship? (Can you copy or improve on their ideas?)
> ❏ Will your company get mentioned in the local and/or trade press, or on radio or TV?
> ❏ Can you afford it? (For every sum you spend on the sponsorship fee, you will need to find the same amount again to exploit your initiative.)
> ❏ Is the sponsorship compatible with the sales image you decided on in Chapter 1?
> ❏ Is the sponsorship exclusive to your company? (Don't share the benefits with anyone else; the publicity and goodwill are diluted.)
>
> If you have answered "Yes" to at least five of these questions, you should consider going ahead.

Insist on value for your money and don't be afraid to be businesslike in dealing with good causes.

> To get the most from sponsorship, apply these rules:
>
> ❏ Demand prominence for your company name and logo.
> ❏ Negotiate the sponsorship fee.
> ❏ Find out if and why anyone has turned down the sponsorship.
> ❏ Get the organisation to guarantee your coverage in advance.
> ❏ Don't sponsor individuals. The returns are too uncertain.

HOW TO PUBLICISE YOUR BUSINESS (AND YOURSELF!)

" Our customers are PC users who tend to throw their equipment away when upgrading. I decided to get them involved in donating the kit to good causes instead. We use our own workshop to refurbish the computers and install them – that's our donation. The customers get as big a buzz as we do, and the photo opportunities are thoroughly exploited. Believe me, these charity organisations really know about publicity! "
– Ed Thorstrom, computer maintenance firm vice-president

In sponsorship, the brand and the logo are the name of the game. Make sure you are organised to exploit visual opportunities by having signs, banners and posters prepared. And check beforehand to make sure all this is acceptable to the media. One brand leader discovered too late that the prissy producer of the TV sports programme covering the national swimming championships dipped the cameras as the swimmers passed below the sponsor's advertising boards.

CYBERSPACE: THE FINAL FRONTIER?

Do you see web sites promoted everywhere and wonder why a business needs such a thing? Surely only kids and anoraks surf the Internet?

There has been a lot of hype surrounding the Internet that stampeded business people into getting in on the act. Nevertheless, a web site is a powerful weapon for a number of reasons.

- ○ It gives the opportunity to reach the ever-increasing armies of high-spending customers who use personal computers at work and at home. And they are not IT nerds. More and more of them get information and make purchases through the web. It is essentially an instant medium.
- ○ A modern, go-ahead company is expected to have a web site as much as email and mobile phones.

IMPROVING PROMOTIONAL PUNCH

○ Finally, the site gives you another opportunity to draw attention to your company and its products by promoting the site as if it were a product in its own right!

> Don't try to re-invent the wheel when developing a web site. Use the text and graphics already in use for other forms of communication – such as an annual report, brochure or proposal form.

The same principles apply to web sites as to brochures, advertising and any other form of promotion: clarity and ease of response. There is no mystery about making the Internet work for you. The ingredients are similar to a brochure, it's just that they have to be presented in a special way since only one page at a time can be seen on a computer screen.

This means that the site visitor must be directed very carefully to the pages they need to see, rather than having to plough hopefully through pages of irrelevant background, not knowing where it leads to. No potential customer has the time or patience to do this!

So the opening – or "home" – page of your site must list the contents of the site and give clear directions based on understanding what the visitor wants.

But the most important element is *what you want to achieve*: maybe a sale. Your site needs to be structured like a very subtle sales conversation that inexorably leads to an application for a proposal, or a sales visit in person, or an email order.

This goal means going beyond the normal logging of numbers of site visitors. You will be able to find out much more about exactly who visits the site by getting them to fill in an email coupon to receive more information from you.

> Always remember that reading a computer screen is generally not as congenial as reading a printed page. The visitor to your site will respond better if layouts are ultra-easy on the eye, avoiding white type on a black background, for instance. Mood is very important on screen, so make the site visit as cheerful as you can, without being fatuous or trivial.

thirty-five

HOW TO PUBLICISE YOUR BUSINESS (AND YOURSELF!)

> *" I made the mistake of not fighting my corner when the IT guys got to work on our web site first. It was a computer thing and responsibilities got confused. The result was a piece of communication not controlled by the marketing department – and unrecognisable as our corporate identity. They even got the logo in the wrong colour! I also thought the text was infantile. I had to take over and start again from scratch. "*
> – **Donald Findlay, marketing manager, toiletries producer**

The graphic designers of cyberspace sometimes call themselves "webmasters". The designer you already know from Chapter 1 may also specialise in web site development, or may be able to recommend a webmaster.

Fix a meeting with at least two different web site designers and ask them for their ideas. Don't expect too much detail, since creative concepts should not be sought without payment.

Ask for addresses of web sites they have developed and surf your way through them to see if they are close to your own cyber-aspirations.

Before these meetings, have every piece of literature, advertising, proposal forms, case histories, annual report and other printed materials available on the table, so the designers can get the full picture in order to make comprehensive suggestions.

Work with the webmaster who has the best grasp of your marketing objectives – including how to make a web site create a sale.

TRICKS OF THE TRADE

— Chapter 4

Coming up in this chapter

Get the best value from advertising
Making the exhibition decision
Make the most of show participation
Exploit face-to-face communications
Make a success of speaker opportunities
Use your products as prizes
Get the most from media competitions
An open day can be a public relations coup
Decide if an open day is right for you

BE YOUR OWN ADVERTISING AGENCY

> Have the complexity and cost of advertising always seemed daunting? Do the mysteries of ad agency creativity and media planning combined with the problem of justifying the cost put you off the whole idea?

Up to now, this book has mainly dealt with publicity based on getting other people, like customers and the media, to write or talk about you. And we have emphasised there are positive aspects of such coverage, especially the credibility and sheer good value. But the two things that "above-the-line" (i.e. paid for) advertising can guarantee is that your message will appear in the media you want (sometimes even on the page you want), on the date you want, with the precise wording and appearance you want.

> To control costs without sacrificing the professionalism that an advertising agency delivers, you need to be your own ad agency. Follow these guidelines:

HOW TO PUBLICISE YOUR BUSINESS (AND YOURSELF!)

- Limit your ad bookings to the very best of the media in your media directory. Your experience of dealing with them will enable you to judge which give the best reach into your market. Remember, the fewer ads you buy, the bigger size you can afford – and size enhances prestige and impact.
- Advertise when you are as sure as you can be that the ad will coincide with editorial publicity, to get maximum clout (but **never** try to use your advertising budget as a lever to get an editorial mention – unless you are arranging an advertorial).
- Make sure your ads claim the same customer benefits as your press release – and use the sales message you worked out in Chapter 1.
- Never pay the full rate for the space – ad sales people are always flexible, even in good times.
- Press for a position early in the journal, and definitely among the editorial pages.
- Get the people who produced your literature to design and process your ad.
- Prepare a media schedule, which is simply a timetable of your ads appearing in your selected media. This stops you missing any deadlines for submitting your copy.

> ❝ Working with our design firm to produce an advertising campaign provided mutual advantages. They welcomed the extra revenue — who wouldn't? — but we, the client, also gained. We benefited from the opportunity to work again with creative people who already understood our business. So this is a partnership that is now delivering regularly. You can't get this support from commissioning the occasional or one-off brochure. ❞
> – **Fred McGovern, packaging manufacturer**

Do a deal with your designers. Get them to book the ad space for you and claim the agency discount, which you can split between you! Check first that the design firm can convince the journal that they qualify for a discount, which will be between 10 and 15%.

TRICKS OF THE TRADE

MAKE A REAL EXHIBITION OF YOURSELF

> Do you find it difficult to tell whether an exhibition is worth the money? On top of the cost of the stand space and the displays you have to take into account the fact that you and your sales people are removed from your normal daily productivity. When the show opens, do you find that hardly anyone is interested in your stand – and the ones who are haven't got the purchasing clout?

Sooner or later (if you haven't already), you will have to make a decision about taking space at a trade or consumer exhibition. Many firms take the negative view that they can't afford *not* to be seen at these shows – it proves they're still in business!

On the positive side, it's a chance to meet customers away from their workplace, to see what the competition are up to – and to get more publicity.

> If the cost of exhibitions makes you hesitate, answer these questions to see if you can justify the expense:
> ❑ Will you meet prospects you would never meet anywhere else?
> ❑ Can the organisers produce convincing evidence that such people will be attending the show?
> ❑ Do you have a new product that can be promoted better in this environment at this time than through, for example, advertising?
> ❑ Can you and/or your staff afford the time away from normal duties?
> ❑ Will your design people produce displays within budget?
> ❑ Have you got plenty of literature to give away?
> ❑ Are you organised to follow-up sales enquiries after the event?
> ❑ Are there conference/seminar opportunities at the show for you to speak about the benefits of your product or service?
> ❑ Will there be a show press office, press previews and reviews of the show and an exhibition newspaper?

thirty-nine

If you decide to take the plunge, do make sure that you give your stand details, including everything that you will be exhibiting, to the press who are covering the event – and to the organiser for the show newspaper.

You may be able to "rent" space on someone else's stand because your work is complementary to theirs, or you may be able to share the cost of your own stand with a supplier, distributor or other business partner.

On the first morning of the exhibition, visit the press office to grab samples of competitors' press material and literature.

" *My PR people hit on a terrific idea to draw attention to my stand. We were launching a new desktop publishing package and they found out that the show organisers were not producing a newspaper. So, over the five days of the show, with the help of a freelance writer, we produced it for them with our own DTP technology! We had record stand traffic because the paper was given to every visitor – with our brand at the top of the front page of every edition. It was also the perfect demonstration of our new product.* "
– Dave North, educational software developer

Whether your stand is large or small, make it easy to walk on to and ensure that there is no clutter. Don't tolerate briefcases and coffee cups left lying around. Arrange a cupboard for literature and equipment.

THE SPEAKER'S SALES OPPORTUNITY

Are you an authority on many professional issues but haven't got the time to write and deliver speeches? Or are you very nervous about presenting in public?

TRICKS OF THE TRADE

Other people's conferences and seminars (usually run by trade associations, exhibition organisers or the media) should be viewed in the same light as media publicity. They offer the same type of opportunity to promote the benefits of your wares – directly or indirectly – to key audiences.

And the dozens, or even hundreds, of listeners will see you as an authority on your subject. They can be met individually during the breaks between sessions, so have plenty of business cards with you!

You don't have to be an international management guru to make an effective presentation. Just be sure of your case – and *rehearse thoroughly*, especially if you are to use audiovisual equipment. One overworked executive just turned up at a conference without having time to check the stage setting and the equipment. It ought to have been a heaven-sent opportunity to be headhunted. Instead, he was humiliatingly seen to be unprepared as he struggled with the projector controls and the order of his slides.

If you are a trade association member, you will get advance information about their events. Other opportunities can be tracked in the trade press and by asking customers which events they attend. As with media and exhibition selection, you have to be sure of certain criteria for the right public appearance.

This list will help you decide which public opportunities to exploit.
- ❏ The organiser can convince you that the right customer or other target audience will attend.
- ❏ This is the only way you can reach a certain group of buyers or influencers.
- ❏ You can afford the time both in preparation and in attendance.
- ❏ You are happy to perform in public – or to take the time to learn to be interesting and convincing.
- ❏ You have something compelling to communicate that is not a blatant sales pitch.
- ❏ You can put together a presentation up to the organisers' standards.

forty-one

HOW TO PUBLICISE YOUR BUSINESS (AND YOURSELF!)

" My PA came across the Financial Times *conference list and saw that their conference on the future of road transport contained world-renowned speakers – but there was one vacant speaker slot. I immediately sold-in a case history about computerised traffic control to reduce pollution. The resulting appearance on the same platform as politicians and business leaders must have made my competitors mad! The contacts I made in that single day will benefit my business for years. "*
– Mitch Kaplan, technical director, worldwide digital traffic control business

To enable your own presentation to stand out during a whole sequence of speeches in a day-long event, generate a little audience participation. For example, before you start talking, ask a question that will get the audience responding – and help you get into your stride.

COMPETITIONS FOR MEDIA IMPACT

Do you think that competitions lower the perceived value of your product and trivialise your marketing strategy?

Competitions are a proven way to get publicity in trade journals, newspapers, radio and TV. The publicity need not look cheap and should fit into any properly planned marketing strategy. The tone of the competition must be dictated by you, so the selection of the media will ultimately ensure the right message.

Obviously, you will need to provide one or more prizes – and the competition should be fun, undemanding and simple in format to help ensure a big response. National media need prizes worth thousands of pounds – a Far Eastern holiday for example – but local press and trade magazines are much more easily satisfied. And you don't have to restrict the competition to just one journal.

TRICKS OF THE TRADE

Offer as many prizes as possible from your own product range – the value to the reader is higher than the cost to you. Therefore, if you are a china manufacturer, the competition could look like this:

WIN A DESIGNER COFFEE MUG WITH
++ ALPINE CERAMICS ++

100 beautiful coffee mugs to be won!

This stylish ceramic coffee mug worth £•• could be yours
in our easy-to-enter competition.
Just look at the two cartoons below.
The pictures may look alike, but there are ten differences.
All you need to do is ring the mistakes, complete the coupon and
send your entry to [name and address of journal].
The first 100 correct entrants will receive a designer mug
made by craftsmen at Alpine Ceramics.

TIPS

HOW TO PUBLICISE YOUR BUSINESS (AND YOURSELF!)

Competitions are usually set up with the media's promotions department, who will establish the rules of the game. Add the contact name to your media directory if you decide to go ahead.

Make sure you are organised to supply the prizes quickly when the winners are known. There is no more certain way to sour media relations than to have readers complaining to the editor that their prize has not turned up!

❝ We decided that there was one DIY magazine read particularly by the specialist market we were after, and contacted them. The editor himself came back to us and suggested a prize each month for the best reader DIY tip sent in. Now, for a power drill prize that costs us peanuts, we get our logo and product in the magazine every issue. ❞
– **Gordon Salter, marketing manager, power tools firm**

Alternatively, you could consider a **reader offer**. Here, you negotiate with the media's promotions people a special price for your product – exclusively to their readers. In exchange, you will get what amounts to a free advertisement proclaiming the offer – as well as guaranteed sales. Additionally, you will get the implied endorsement of your product quality simply by being associated with the journal.

OPEN YOUR DOORS TO BUYERS AND FIXERS

Have you been tempted by the idea of inviting all and sundry to a party, but been put off by the thought of your tatty premises and sloppy staff?

An open day will give you the opportunity to meet and impress many different audiences in a single event. And it could also be the trigger to improve the working environment and professionalism of your people.

TRICKS OF THE TRADE

An open day would be expensive, time-consuming and counter-productive if you cannot meet most of these criteria:
- ❏ You have a reason to open your doors, like the inauguration of your premises, an anniversary, new machinery or building, or a new division.
- ❏ Your premises are a reasonable showcase for your business.
- ❏ Your displays, presentation materials and skills are of a high enough standard.
- ❏ You are prepared to organise and cater for either a single large group or several smaller ones.
- ❏ A large enough number of your customers are within easy travelling distance.
- ❏ You can supplement the numbers with "fixers" – people like local councillors, your MP, community business leaders, consultants/analysts, the media and others who can influence your business prospects beneficially.

A manufacturer of point-of-sale equipment decided to rearrange his premises as a spoof golf course, with points accumulated by visitors answering a mixture of professional and general knowledge questions at key stages or "holes" round the course. The 19th hole, of course, made the effort worthwhile!

> " We had just installed some new, very high-tech (and very expensive) printing machines and decided this was the best opportunity we had ever had to demonstrate our long-term commitment to our marketplace. Most customers had never visited us before and had no idea how advanced and complex our set-up is. Getting the actual machine-minders involved in technical explanations also helped internal relations and pride in the job. Now our customers have a greater understanding of how we deliver – literally, an accurate picture of our business. The positive feedback we got after the event convinced us that we had to do this more often. "
> – **Michael Byrne, printing company CEO**

HOW TO PUBLICISE YOUR BUSINESS (AND YOURSELF!)

If you commit yourself to an open day, decide who is responsible for what activity, and when, and follow this checklist for organising the event:

Open day organisation chart

Activity	Responsibility	Date
Staff briefing		
Invitation list		
Invitation letter/card		
Telephone follow-up		
Photographer		
Press release		
Name badges		
Displays		
Presentation		
Guided tour		
Signing-in book		
Catering		
Programme		
Parking		
Toilets		
Signs		
Welcome/reception		
Gift		
Closing/departure		
Staff debriefing		

SEE THE RESULTS

Chapter 5

Coming up in this chapter

Simple and effective ways to measure publicity success
Lessons from case histories

EVALUATING YOUR PUBLICITY PROGRAMME

Do you know instinctively how well your publicity activities are doing? Do lots of people say they have read about you, but you've never got round to getting hold of the articles? Or was it your ads they saw? Do you know what people read about you?

The public relations world agonises over the question of evaluation. Many companies have exploited this competitive anxiety with complex and often unintelligible computerised measurement systems. Still, the printouts look good when presented to the client. And, naturally, they cost much more than old-fashioned, common-sense methods.

You should not think about spending any real money on evaluation because your publicity objectives, as described in the preceding chapters, are simple and therefore easy to measure.

So you won't even need a press cuttings service, for instance, unless you are involved in a national programme reaching more media than you can monitor yourself (and even then, you'll have to do a lot of chasing – press cuttings agencies are not very reliable). But make sure you are organised to do this yourself. Brief a member of staff whose responsibility it is to make sure you know how well the publicity is doing.

Don't get involved with expensive research about your image among your target market. It will cost more than the publicity itself.

forty-seven

HOW TO PUBLICISE YOUR BUSINESS (AND YOURSELF!)

" The thing that finally convinced me not to hire one PR firm was the evaluation scheme they presented. The people we saw made such a big deal of it in their presentation, as if they were worried that their promotional ideas weren't up to scratch – or we didn't like their people. And what we were shown was a bunch of mysterious charts with jargon that Einstein couldn't interpret. "
— **Mark Lewis, office supplies retail chain**

How to measure the success of your publicity

- ❏ If you don't subscribe to a publication you are expecting coverage in, get the journalist to send you a copy of the relevant issue.
- ❏ You can record the odd radio and TV broadcast yourself.
- ❏ Many trade magazines provide free a reader response service about companies they mention. These sales leads are sent to you to follow up.
- ❏ Ask enquirers where they read or heard about you.
- ❏ Build attitude assessment into your ongoing customer relationships. Just keep asking what they think of you.
- ❏ Are you getting coverage in the media you originally selected in Chapter 2?
- ❏ Are the articles (or tapes) really promoting the customer benefit messages you identified in Chapter 1?
- ❏ How many and what standard of visitors came to your exhibition stand, conference presentation, open day or sponsored event?
- ❏ How many entries did the press competition deliver? Have you got the names and addresses of the entrants for direct mail?
- ❏ Are you getting significant sales enquiries through the web site?

" Doing our own media monitoring really focused my mind on the wastage in our press list. The burden of having to follow up dozens of journals made me reassess exactly who we were sending material to. We quickly stripped out about half the list containing small or obscure magazines and now the process is quite manageable. "
— **Donna Biss, publisher**

forty-eight

SEE THE RESULTS

CASE HISTORY: CASSIE'S CAKES

Step 1: Deciding what's special

Cassie's Cakes was set up by Cassandra Deft-Touch. In deciding to launch the enterprise, she persuaded her sister, Alexandra, to join her. They are based in Bath, England, and the premises comprise a small shop and a kitchen. Cassie's Cakes are handmade, primarily for special occasions, and are sold direct both to private and trade customers, as well as through the shop, which also serves as a showcase.

With their cooking and design skills, the sisters recognised that there was a market for exclusive, top-quality cakes for people with money to spare. After all, they had both been asked in the past to supply many society gatherings.

In deciding what was special about their product, they wrote down the words "quality, taste, exclusive, handmade, special". And Cassie's Cakes would be marketed as "cakes for people with taste".

Step 2: Defining the market

Their market partly decided itself. Most of the cakes they produced would be bought by people like their comfortably off friends. However, the sisters also needed to sell to hotels and function rooms, as well as to people who would be prepared to pay more for a birthday or a wedding.

For publicity purposes they defined their market specifically. They targeted women in the upper middle class, aged between 25 and 35: the most likely to be involved in weddings and parties, as well as birthdays for themselves and young children. The other important market was catering managers.

Geographically, they decided to restrict their activity to Bath and the surrounding 10-mile radius where there was the greatest concentration of people they wanted to sell to. They also knew that major centres like Bristol or Chippenham had their own specialist cake firms. In any case, they were concerned that they should be able meet local demand efficiently.

HOW TO PUBLICISE YOUR BUSINESS (AND YOURSELF!)

Step 3: Designing and printing

The sisters commissioned a graphic designer to produce a basic range of stationery, a simple leaflet suitable for mailing to catering managers, a price list and shop displays. The visual impact was conveyed by the logo, which appeared to be written in icing sugar, while the symbol they chose was the icing tool itself.

Step 4: Creating the media directory

They selected the *Bath Evening Chronicle*, with its strong women's page, the county magazine, a group of local weeklies and two local radio stations, HTV and BBC TV West. They couldn't find any journal specific to the local catering trade, but reasoned that catering professionals also read the local press!

Step 5: Getting the media interested

The sisters decided that, although Cassie's Cakes was a new company with a quality product, those reasons alone were not strong enough to get lots of publicity. What they needed was an idea with impact that would show themselves as well as their product.

So, they baked a very special cake for a very special occasion. A local church was approaching its 500th anniversary, therefore they made a replica of it in cake form, complete with 500 candles, and presented it to the vicar to raffle for the church tower fund.

Rather than merely sending out a picture with a press release, they arranged an unveiling to which the media were invited in a photo call.

> "To celebrate 500 years of St Michael's Church, Cassie's Cakes, the new cake makers of Bath, have made a giant birthday cake, which will be presented to the vicar, the Rev. John Smith. The cake, which is a six-feet high replica of the church, has so many candles that the church choir has been enlisted to blow them out. After the birthday ceremony, the cake will be on display at the Cassie's Cakes shop, where it will be raffled – the proceeds going to the church tower fund."

SEE THE RESULTS

The following press release was also mailed to media unable to attend the unveiling:

For further information, please contact
Cassandra Deft-Touch, Cassie's Cakes
(address, tel., email & fax).

LOCAL CHURCH GETS ITS OWN BIRTHDAY CAKE

A six-feet high cake made as a replica of St Michael's Church in Northchester was presented today [date] to the vicar by its makers, Cassie's Cakes of Bath. The cake was made to commemorate the church's 500th birthday, and it took the full church choir to blow out the candles.

Cassandra Deft-Touch who, with her sister Alexandra, runs the newly launched Cassie's Cakes, said,"The cake took us three weeks to make and weighs nearly 100 pounds. It used up 10,000 currants and sultanas, two miles of iced piping and twenty pounds of sugar."

After the presentation, the cake was put on display at Cassie's Cakes shop, 22 High Street, Bath, where it will be raffled during the next month, the proceeds going to the St Michael's Church tower fund.

Commented the vicar, The Rev. John Smith, "We were delighted to receive such a wonderful and unusual birthday present. I now hope that the people of Bath will get very involved in the raffle so we can begin restoration of the tower, which is the most beautiful example of late medieval architecture".

ENDS

Results

All of the papers that received the photo call attended on the day, along with one each of the TV and radio stations. The newspapers all used the photographs they took, mentioning Cassie's Cakes and including the sisters in the picture. The TV station broadcast a full minute of choirboys blowing out the candles while the radio station also invited Cassandra on to their morning show to talk about the event.

HOW TO PUBLICISE YOUR BUSINESS (AND YOURSELF!)

Building for the future

Cassandra and Alexandra have made good contacts with the media who attended the photo call and have fixed up interviews on the women's pages of the papers that carried their story. They have also stayed in touch with the radio station with a view to Cassandra having her own weekly five-minute spot on their women's programme.

Alexandra had the idea of mailing copies of the newspaper pictures to local catering managers, and commissions have already been received. Also, the sisters have promoted themselves through demonstrations at Women's Institute meetings.

As a result of a high-profile launch, intelligently followed up, Cassie's Cakes has become instantly established and is busy making both cakes and profits.

SEE THE RESULTS

CASE HISTORY: DIRECT ELECTRONICS

Step 1: Deciding what's special

Simon Suretouch, the boss of a new company called Direct Electronics, used to be the marketing boss of a much larger rival, Turgid Components. It was while he was working for them that he hit upon the idea that made him start his own company. He realised that what Turgid's customers wanted (but no supplier provided) was direct sales supported by a customer care service.

So Simon put this proposition to his bank manager and other financial backers, using as evidence the researched opinions of many customers he had spoken to in the past.

Bypassing the distributor-based tradition of his industry enabled Direct Electronics to make this claim in their sales proposition: "Faster delivery, better value and more trust". This powerful sales message was also featured prominently in the new Direct Electronics web site. Now Simon needed to decide who he was going to tell his story to.

Step 2: Defining the market

Deciding who would buy his product was no problem for such a marketing professional as Simon, but he knew he had to prioritise in the early days in order not to create more demand than he could supply.

So he decided initially to stick to the UK market which, unlike larger overseas potential customers, comprised many small to medium-sized companies, few of whom had complex buying processes or internal advisers and influencers. The buying decision would often be made by the managing director, who would in many cases also be a technician, in consultation with his financial chief.

And he knew that large numbers of his customers were located in regions favoured by electronics firms, like Scotland's "Silicon Glen" or the M4 Corridor in southern England, so he also needed a regional dimension to his publicity plan.

HOW TO PUBLICISE YOUR BUSINESS (AND YOURSELF!)

Step 3: Creating the media directory

With a strong story to tell and a clear audience to listen to it, media selection was vital to the success of Direct Electronics.

Because his customers were all in the same trade and spread nationally, Simon decided he had to get publicity in the eight or nine electronics magazines read by his customers and to include the specialist correspondents of national newspapers, as well as about a dozen influential freelance electronics industry writers.

To this list he added the business editors of Scottish daily papers and M4 Corridor dailies like the *Reading Evening Post* and *Swindon Evening Advertiser*. For good measure, he included half a dozen county business journals from these regions.

Even without radio and television (which were unlikely to be worth targeting in year one), with the inclusion of the firm's own regional daily and two weekly newpapers, the Direct Electronics media directory had nearly 50 entries. Of course, there would only be time for less than a dozen of these to receive priority treatment, but Simon knew that his customers would be getting his message from all directions.

Step 4: Getting the media interested

This is the press release that Simon wrote (note the use of research and the unique sales proposition as well as the opportunity given to the quoted customer to reach his own audience: his shareholders):

For further information, please contact Simon Suretouch, Managing Director, Direct Electronics
(address, tel., email, website & fax).

DIRECT SALES FIRM GIVES ELECTRONICS INDUSTRY NEW DEAL

A new company called Direct Electronics was launched today, [date], to enable makers of electronics goods, for the first time, to benefit from buying components direct from the manufacturer.

fifty-four

SEE THE RESULTS

Research conducted by Direct Electronics showed that the vast majority of electronics goods manufacturers would welcome a radical alternative to the traditional distributor system of component supply.

This need has now been met by Direct Electronics who claim not only to provide faster delivery and better value, but also greater commitment to the performance of their components within the customer's production environment.

The new company's commitment to service is exemplified by the establishment of a Direct Hotline. This link provides a 24-hour component ordering and "troubleshooter" service to customers right through production shifts, day and night. The entire product range can be assessed and ordered via the web address (www.directelec.com).

Sid Saleschart, Managing Director of microprocessor manufacturer Techprofits plc, commented, "I see this development as a new deal for the industry. As one of Direct's first customers, we are expecting improved quality and productivity as a result of this initiative by a major supplier, which can only be good news for our shareholders."

Direct Electronics' Managing Director, Simon Suretouch, said, "Our long experience of working with the electronics manufacturing sector made it clear to us that direct component sales and service must be the way forward for the supply industry. Vendors and finished goods makers will all benefit from this major change in customer service."

ENDS

The story was significant enough for Suretouch to hold the release until a series of press briefings could be called.

He had decided that he could publicise the new company purely on the strength of a media relations project and therefore did not put aside money for advertising.

Simon sent the following invitation letter to the 20 most important media and, if he got a refusal, extended the list to lower priority media, one by one:

HOW TO PUBLICISE YOUR BUSINESS (AND YOURSELF!)

Dear (Editor's/Journalist's name),

INVITATION TO THE LAUNCH OF DIRECT ELECTRONICS, [PLACE AND DATE]

I would like to invite you to the launch of a new company formed to provide a radically new components supply deal for the electronics industry.

Our long experience and research throughout the electronics industry has shown that the need for this development is overdue.

At the launch, you will have the opportunity to meet me and at least one major manufacturing customer to answer your questions. You will join a small press group without competitor journalists present.

The following times are available for you to choose from for your visit to our factory and offices: ...

We will call you in a couple of days to see which time you prefer.

Yours sincerely,

**Simon Suretouch
Managing Director**

The invitation worked and most of the primary press were able to attend. With careful management, this combination of media was achieved for each of four press groups: electronics trade journal, local newspaper, national daily press technology correspondent and freelance journalist.

Important media who could not attend interviewed Simon on the phone in between group meetings and the rest of the media were mailed the press pack containing the release.

SEE THE RESULTS

Results

The launch received in-depth favourable coverage in all the important journals. Each carried the sales message and, together with additional publicity in the second priority media (who were also mailed the press pack), generated enormous customer interest, including numerous direct sales leads from reader response cards sent by the trade press.

Building for the future

Naturally, the immediate business priority for Direct Electronics was to meet the demand created by publicity from a successful launch.

But the labour-intensive part of the publicity programme was complete. Simon was able to build on the recognition he had achieved by ensuring he met key journalists two or three times a year, offering them a customer case history to publish, and negotiating the occasional advertorial.

Additionally, he made it his business to speak at electronics industry conferences where the subject of customer care was relevant, including the Electronica exhibition held each spring where he invested in stand space.

Now that Direct Electronics' production line and track record have become established, Simon is considering an open day at which he will, in a special press gathering, announce overseas marketing plans for year two.

Titles Available in the 60 Minutes Success Skills Series

1 901306 35 6	*Winning Sales Letters*, John Frazer-Robinson
1 901306 32 1	*Influence and Succeed!*, Fiona Elsa Dent
1 901306 22 4	*Super Communications the NLP Way*, Russell Webster
1 901306 27 5	*Building Customer Loyalty*, John Frazer-Robinson
1 901306 25 9	*Effective Direct Mail*, John Frazer-Robinson
1 901306 26 7	*High Performance Sales Management*, John Frazer-Robinson
1 901306 28 3	*Mastering Motivation*, John Frazer-Robinson
1 901306 20 8	*Successful Internet Marketing*, Veronica Yuill
1 901306 13 5	*Find that Job!*, Calum Roberts
1 901306 10 0	*Successful Marketing*, Mike Levy
1 901306 12 7	*Super Selling*, Russell Webster
1 901306 11 9	*Successful Interviewing*, Mike Levy
1 901306 06 2	*Planning your Business* Richard Burton
1 901306 05 4	*Painless Business Finance*, Mark Allin
1 901306 08 9	*Managing People for the First Time*, Ron Bracey
1 901306 07 0	*Effective Appraisal Skills*, Graham Taylor
1 901306 00 3	*Get yourself Organised!*, Mike Levy
1 901306 02 X	*Maximise your Time*, Ron Bracey
1 901306 01 1	*Become Assertive*, James Fleming

All at just £4.99 or local equivalent!

These books should be available at good booksellers around the world. In case of difficulty, contact **David Grant** for details of local stockists at:

80 Ridgeway, Pembury, Kent TN2 4EZ, UK
tel/fax +44 [0]1892 822886
Email GRANTPUB@aol.com